# "Don't Tell Me Trees
Don't Talk"
and Other Poems

# "Don't Tell Me Trees Don't Talk" and Other Poems

Jesse Bier

Lewisburg
Bucknell University Press
London: Associated University Presses

Associated University Presses
440 Forsgate Drive
Cranbury, NJ 08512

Associated University Presses
16 Barter Street
London WC1A 2AH, England

Associated University Presses
P.O. Box 338, Port Credit
Mississauga, Ontario
Canada L5G 4L8

The paper used in this publication meets the requirements of the American National Standard for Permanence of Paper for Printed Library Materials Z39.48–1984.

**Library of Congress Cataloging-in-Publication Data**

Bier, Jesse.
  "Don't tell me trees don't talk", and other poems / Jesse Bier.
    p.  cm.
  ISBN 0-8387-5343-4 (alk. paper)
  I. Title.
PS3552.I3562D6   1997
811'.54—dc21                      96-44564
                                    CIP

For
Nathan, Jordan, Benjamin, Madeleine, and Elliot

# Contents

# Acknowledgments


"Tree of Northern Lights," *Carleton Miscellany*.

"This Now is Blazing Cold" and "Between Garrison Junction and Alberton, Montana," *Contempora*.

"Transport of Love" and "Sonnet: The Solecism of Your Smile ... ," *Discourse*.

"Netted Trout West of Missoula" and "Can't Make Up My American Mind," *The Eclectic Muse*.

"Close-Call for the End of the World," *Jeopardy*.

"Yom Kippur in Montana," *Jewish Currents*.

"Tropic Trees," "Spacesurfers," and "The Frogs of Kauai," *Kaimana: Literary Arts of Hawaii*.

"Hyde Park," *New Republic*.

"Fleeting Thoughts in Montana at 48° below Zero, with Wind-Chill, at the Age of 66," *Parnassus Literary Journal*.

"Better Not Go," "'Flee fly flow from,'" "Hear Ye and Harken ... ," "In These Mountains," "All Oceans Beat upon Montana," "The Fifty-sixth Year of My Shepherd," "Mary Ann at Sweeney Creek," and "The One That Got Away," *Trestle Creek Review*.

"The Skunk" and "Don't Tell Me Trees Don't Talk," *The Trumpeter*.

"Raincoatéd Victory" and "February: American Christmas," *Virginia Quarterly Review*.

"The Cook Islands Christian Church, Raratonga" and "The Last Horse and My Father," *West Branch*.

# Section I

# Netted Trout West of Missoula

This eye may be compared to nothing else. The fish
gazes wild, flattens as he comes sideways to hand,
is the thing itself, while I reach for my net to land
him. All other fear must be compared to this:
fixed and gelid eye, naked stare the fisherman cannot miss,
the look straight into death. I am unmanned,
my heart thudding in my throat as I stand
to lift him in the soft cage of corded earth. The rapids hiss,
spilling into the pool where he was hooked. I let line slack.
One second or two untick, without a sound, not even the roaring jet
   boom
heard before. O, I saw the stricken quiver shiver down his spine.
Suddenly world-sounds (the rapids, a coughing car) come back.
It was not self-identifying fear but the terror of losing him made my
   doom,
why my heart thudded so. Now the distant jet drones its high hollow
   whine.

# The Fifty-sixth Year of My Shepherd

Whining hoarsely the wheeze he whistles in his throat,
old Shep lumbers over the lawn grass,
sits at these knees, resigns his ripped head to my lap. The toy poodle
   leaps
at the shepherd's ruff, worrying that deep cut in the coat
just below the left ear. The wound weeps
blood—one of the four humours. To suffer this diminutive sass
after a wild locked fight
with mastiffs up the valley unsettles the big fellow's affections.
I pluck the pup and hold him high. It's only right
to rescue old dogs from light-weights; the shepherd poses no
   objections.

Because that's what he wanted me to do in the first place,
wasn't it? Sits now, satisfied. I place the other, rascal fluff, on my knee.
Now the big one perceives I have understood him, his face
shows it to interpreters of dog yawns and slavering tongues. I know
   him. And him me.
I don't claim I understood just at the second
he wanted me to. Maybe, after quick response, *then* I understood. No
   matter.
I mean, I'm God to this eight-year-old watchdog, who has reckoned
such ever since his coming here eight years ago—rather
like fifty-six, times'd by seven, in human terms. That's old to be still
   believing.

He's the important one of the two, on guard at nights even in
   Montana cold.
The poodle, on the other hand (or knee), is not serious canine mettle.
   But he's never leaving
well enough alone, always up and at the old
one, whom he takes for a great mother and father both. For his part,
   the shepherd trusts
me with large and similar devotion. (So we grant Omniscience up a
   scale
of being.) Nonetheless, eyeing me askance just now, he wonders how I
   happened to fail

him yesterday, how in the world I didn't know
he was up the valley in a three-way dogfight, pursuing his old lusts
at 3:20 P.M.? why I didn't fully manifest or show
fantastic powers by hurling the black mastiff who had him under
the ear to Limbo, or Wood's Gulch at least? God's way
seems limited. At the last, he accepts that. Never mind lax thunder,
it's enough I demonstrate welcome and appreciate appeals today.
He won't like the penance of antiseptic on the wound,
though. I predetermine it. But that's divinity
for you, working in mysterious ways, suddenly liable to confound
the simplest trust with sharpest sting. (My analogy to Infinity.)

    What's there more to moralize? There are no absolutely dumb
beasts, or perfect masters. We all struggle through numb
reasons to partial understanding and willed communion. I am myself
   part
shepherd also and poodle too? That goes without saying,
I won't draw it out. We're after the heart
of another matter. I've let the pup down and he's playing
now with the other's paw gently, having caught the mood.
In this vale (so to speak), on this ball of rock and water, in this wood
of sunsplit pine and quaking aspen, that's worth notation
so long as we don't exceed ourselves in mutual elation.

    The truth is, I caught the old dog's meaning just barely
that minute ago. Preoccupied or otherwise distracted.
Now, if *that's* God, it's a notion fairly
phrased and I agree—though our nonsensical sun freeze compacted
soon or later—and dogfights and gradual comprehension come to
   nothing at all.
Nevertheless, this shepherd is devout: exquisite ears stand pertly at my
   call.

# "Flee fly flow from"
# (for James Agee)

Flee fly flow from this week-end driver
up the Madison. Tug, you calves, at the teats
of you cows: you will have it, you will have it, and bleat
your pleasure. Yet we will have you, we the givers
of clean pasture will seize the fat and brand the lean, none will thrive
beyond our deceitful appetite. But tender shoots of wheat
still my carnivorous heart, sweet rills of tiny water are other feats
of spring. I am the Sunday traveler, soothed journeyman, shriver
of sins and discomforts. . . . Dumb brute beasts, lolling to feed
in these fields, hear the silent sirens scream: leap barbed wire and rails
of your concentrated camps of grass: all the many or only the some
of you: jump this river, wade the Missouri Breaks, stampede
to Canada! Hypocrite speedster, worse than your guards, I am the ogre
   to quail
flee fly and flow from.

# Time Out of Mind

Get the horse back in the stable, hay crammed along rafters and high
  in the loft,
motes and splinters in the air so thick that even the horse (you said)
  might cough.
Get the big dog barking at something, or nothing, maybe a turn of the
  spring wind.
Get you, and you me, and time out of mind.

Get back April: lily of the valley, lilac (your favorite) and Indian
  paintbrush.
Get dawns before everybody else is up, earth stock-still before the
  morning rush
on the county road, people on the move, to work, to seek, to lose, to
  find.
Get you, and you me, and time out of mind.

Get back one certain May, our kids flinging to the bus, all skittery for
  school;
get them coming home in late afternoon, cheeks persimmon-red,
  kissable and cool.
Get a hollow-sky'd June (as you named it), the clean and high-domed
  kind.
Get you, and you me, and time out of mind.

Can get back anything I want just by concentration, remembering
hard (though you call it my habit of julying instead of novembering).
I know that. Why am I deaf and blind
to any travail then? cleaving to you (and you to me) in time out of
  mind.

# Cross Country

Up ahead the column of cloud lifts a mushroom dome, broader
than we remember. Is the big sky bombing Stevens-
ville, Trapper's Peak and the Bitterroot daughter
mountains to the south? Fallout is snow radiated from heaven,
pure and unadulterated. Here there is no death.
For now, kinesis and release that only the hang glider
can rival and know. We slide the trail, see our quick and plosive breath,
watch our ski tips: complex laminated plastic for long striders
in the new wilderness. Dread freedom, these are our tools,
too. West of Johnson Bell are planes, kindred to Enola Gay,
dropping retardant or search-and-rescue teams. We are not only fools
but may save the woods, find a lone crippled hunter who's lost his way.
We are our own instruments, for good or ill:
To follow loth, follow loathe, or follow the jubilant will.

# The Truth about Cherry Picking

Pick, pick, pick: one after one after one: pick and pick:
take two, then three, grip four or more, a whole hand
ful. Start slow, then quick, quicker quick
and quicker. Some avid demon makes each finger a wand
of deft and nimble greed. Now a palm, a clutch
flings cherries to the pail. One and two and that small ball
of three and four or more. Wait, wait: overmuch,
some too many are quashed to cherry pulp. Remember, not all
will go to general pies and jams. Choose control,
one after one, clean and singular, for simple eating, pith
on pit and pit on stem. Pull by stem ends, without a toll
of sterile strips the tree can do nothing with
for bud or blossom or fruition. Keep in mind
next year. Harvest is no more furious than lazy.
Go back from clutch and palm to one and two, precise and kind.
Resist momentum and the avid demon. In all ways don't go crazy.

# The Skunk

In the live trap the skunk lies quiet,
rummages around and shifts occasionally front to back.
He seems perplexed, not panicked. It is daylight now,
time for sleep anyway. He thinks, maybe, that when
waking under pinpoint mountain stars, this caged show
of confinement will have given way and he'll be free again,
scrounging bird feeder sunflower seeds and the rest of his diet.
But he will not feed again, see this very night, follow a track
anywhere. Because the trapper man is coming and will throw
a wide poncho over the cage and him, probably while he sleeps,
deepening his dream, and then will carry him off, stow
him behind his pickup.
      Skunks smell bad only on occasion,
but are not bad. (You can't do much about reputation).
They look for grubs and night crawlers on the lawn,
rooting and divoting it up especially toward dawn,
but they are not otherwise bad. They keep down field mice.
And they themselves would be in balance if we only
had the coyotes and foxes and wolves we once had in these parts.
But these parts are suburban now, and the trapper comes, creeps
to the little cage, hoods it, folds the poncho all about,
carries the trap to the end of his tail pipe, takes out
flexible hose, snugs it to the exhaust, then starts
the engine and asphyxiates the skunk. In a trice.
I am grateful for that. At the same time, of course, something bitter
and hollow seizes my chest. (Is that my heart?) Also a lonely
feeling. It turns out it was not a he
at all but a heftily pregnant she
who would have given a whole litter
more of skunks to share this acreage with. Just before
being hooded, she was momentarily pungent. The aroma
spreads now, overcomes the other heavy sweet smell of carbon
 monoxide,
hangs on decisively, and will last five days. Her coma
will last longer. Still everything's been clean, without blood or gore.
Nevertheless, the carrigana bushes are offended, the spruce
and fuschia are offended, and the grass, skirting near and wide,

is offended. I permanently put away that trap I've used to catch and
  relocate
pesky squirrels. Neither are they pesky.
Nor the nimble nosed mouse who hides his whiskers
in the barn. What I want is truce.
Going after one is going after the other, it's too risky.
But a tender conscience is tender too late.
It is no illusion that the carriganas sway down,
that the spruce is a darkening blue, that the fuschia crown
leans over the grass, which whispers, whispers.

# Mary Ann at Sweeney Creek

What do you see, Mary Ann,
what do you see in the grass?

*Furrows of a faint wheel track*
*where wagon trains would pass.*

What do you see, Mary Ann,
there at the edge of the wood?

*The grove where the wagons*
*    disappeared*
*and a shadow where the last one*
*    stood.*

What do you see, Mary Ann,
as the blood-red sun goes down?

*A low lit lantern in the canvas loft,*
*swaying—now it's gone.*

And what do you hear, Mary Ann,
from that wind-strewn, echoing ground?

*Where a babe lies buried,*
*mourners weeping by the mound.*

What do you hear, Mary Ann,
sounding softly from the trees.

*Life going on: sighs of a pretty girl*
*for one she wishes to please.*

What do you hear, Mary Ann,
as evening falls fast, then faster?

*Hoofbeats of the chestnut bay*
*ridden by the wagon master,*
*and the snort*
*of the horse he reins up short,*
*not wanting to ride on past her.*

What made you see, Mary Ann,
and made you hear beside?

> *A fond imagination*
> *and fonder feelings deep inside.*

O something stronger, Mary Ann,
came in among your boasts.

> *Don't tell me, sir,*
> *what they were—*
> *were they?—they were—ghosts.*

# In These Mountains

1

      Heat haze or the optical illusion of sound,
the vibrant horizon strums.
In any dawn we hear hoof-beats across buttes,
a rhythm of blood in our temples like drums.
The wind plays on Montana grain, lithe lutes
of melody grass.
              Listen, though: that hum along wires wound
from tree to leafless tree—grieving metronomes. Wailing lines
intermit the landscape, score the wind, keen a dim lament.
(Remember totem poles hewed from pines?)

     And wood-burners: great dark
tepees sending their smoke signals high up the center flue.
The sullied plume of victory—or alarm, stark
alarm? Incinerated Indians and the woods. Do we construe
ourselves as having won those savage wars, and this sawdust from the
   broken
dolls of limp enemies only? Our skulls shrink, hung at our own belts!
   The rents
of smoke proceed from burnt-out promises, spoken
by livid ghosts who will not lie.
                 Here's more armed
vision: irrigation geysers sputter like artillery across the farmed
battlefields of the Bitterroot. The river level ominously lessens.
Each year squadrons of Canada geese fly on—elsewhere—trumpeting
   tawdry lessons
of attrition. Fateful facts as well as mourning mood.

2

      Forced march: our afternoon's hike to some upland wood
for a view of the country in the round, as it were—
I mean to say "as is" and spare the whimsy. Look then: a stillness of
   late day-
light and organdy clouds no one can desecrate. Silhouette of fir
like lace work embroidered on that canyon ridge, a last ray
of paling sun making filigrees of distant purple spruce trees.

From this switchback straight out and down:
strewn wheat bundles on ranch land, like buttons on
plaid pleated skirts of field. (Earth is handsome still, pieced in a gown
made for her by husbandmen.) A stir of hushed breeze
rustles the bear grass, whispering sibilance, occasionless to grieve.
Evening headlights on the old logging road across the valley appear and
    disappear, gone
before we guess exactly: will o' the wisp in a diminished grove of trees.
I believe! I believe!


3
Descent. A swoop of bat's wing. Hold
your hair against premonition. Now there, off the track:
late-blooming lavender brightens from the forest floor,
upthrust blue-lit chandelier . . . almost luminous, we're told,
at just this hour of day this time of year. On our way back
that's pretty and useful light to go by, proper poesy.
—Did you feel the sudden gust? Nothing. Night rising, nothing more—
The sides of these old hills seem animate in lengthening shadow,
leonine hides twitching in the rosy
witch-light of evening that comes on flushed before the cougar dark
    will follow.
        There! feel it grate under the heel? See it now
glitter in the dimming path: spattered glass senseless on the trail?
And there! bright barrow of beer-cans—the fired, flung casings of how-
itzer breweries. Crushed paper like crumpled white flags of surrender.
    In the undergrowth
scattered conundrums of every kind in a riddle of waste. This is the
    part
of Squalid Peak that named it to me. (Such facts smart
patriots of the imagination and lash us to words' revenge. Who's loth
to be reminded this is God's Living Room or fail
to draw conclusions? Unnatural anthems and hymns.)
Nothing's changed. We leached
    the sod, left bison offal on the plains
for coyotes and magpies, or general decay. O! bleached
in the pure prairie air! Who is it complains
that Nature works roundabout through human indirection?
These cans will surely rust. Like the hunkered bygone cars
we pile to shore up river banks. What section

27

of the country is not rife with oxidation under these steady stars?

4

Render unto Custer what is Custer's, and our garbage to God. But if He
    will not dispose
of it as soon as we wish and allows us to wallow
in what we have wrought? Coming and going, we meet
ourselves then and now, now as then, and pay our sins in throes
of mis-giving. Slashed pine and willow,
fuming relicts of a remnant rape. Beer-can wedding rings and diamond
    chips
of splintered glass. (Rage wars with scorn, the whips
of flagellant derision answer self-defeat.)
Lions leap to Manitoba. Our souls bleat.
We never conquered the land, it conquered us. Redmen have
these scalps! Our brains shrivel. Loveless laughter of
the dispossessed, we are punished by what we are.
Our penitence a coon-skin cap where our heads were.
How strong
    the hay smells: heavy-sweet this far
from fields we're coming back to. (In the night nothing's wrong
again.) The horizon blurs, hooded at the end of the draw.
No lute wind or wailing wires. Hushed truce. Above, free and petulant,
    crows caw.

# All Oceans Beat upon Montana

The wind shifts Mediterranean in these woods. Some
sea off New Zealand whooshes through the spruce, combing and
   soughing like
surf. Plangent pines sigh into sand.
The Atlantic drums down canyons, pours over high land
and tight horizons. Dike after clashing dike
of clouds holds a blue flood from red mesas and rimrocks.
Bering beach-heads tune the tree tops.
Hot headlands and frozen fjords boom out of fast-
nesses of rainforest and glacial moraine. Clattering all-colored
weatherbirds soar.

Swelling crescendos foam from
an aboriginal floor of conch-skull: soundings of shell-bone.
What's done
inside these hemispheres is music past
geography. Firs like lyres!
At timberline thought-waves crash to crystal, sibilant spray aspires
to quartz. One singing coast of spume and rock, one high visionary
   shore!

# Don't Tell Me Trees Don't Talk

I tell her, they sigh
they positively breathe a sigh of relief or husky thanks.
"Who? the carrigana?" Yes, and the heretofore high
honeysuckle bushes. "Even the spruce wind-break, and our banks
of lilac." I remember from the time before.
I light out with any stick that's handy, or an old
long broom-handle, and whack the snow off them. It's a chore
that a sudden April blizzard bestows on Montana, rain turned cold
and heavy, wet snow prodigious in the trees and on the land.
Nothing can hold up under the sodden burden, withstand
the weight of white—thickening, thickening. Enough to crack these trees,
    trees,
weeping worse than any willow, curling to the ground,
pleading: Pity me, or: I can't bear it, and: I'll freeze
for sure, and split under this ice-skin. My back is bound
to break (they say), Our limbs are splayed.


I hurry out, my heart already pumping.
It's not the exercise. It's that pity, for this joke played
by one more late-acting winter. I smack hard, laden branches jumping
out and up, and free. I swear I hear the rest:
Me too, me too! *Save me.* For crying out loud,
get a move on. . . . But I'm doing my best,
flailing them up and away. (Of course they don't cry
out loud, but I hear them: whimpering, bough'd
over, all waiting their turn.) "I'm coming, I'm coming," I say and whip
the tangled branches—waling on them—on the snow,
on clicking ice. I slash, pound, thwack, cut, clip,
pummel empty air sometimes, then slap an upper branch bending low.
I hear the soft boom of arboreal snow avalanching down
around me, and *on* me: hat and head white, ears frosted but tuned to that sound
    that sound
I hear (helping the next and then the next and the next) as I go by,
sighing softly that resilient after-sigh
of release: for one more chance at unencumbered spring.
Oh you (they say), Oh man. Just the thing
to straighten my spine, coil back my limbs. Oh good! Now leave

me be, I can resist any new onslaught and grow
like anything. . . . Ah, they sigh so.

"They don't sigh," she says. "You're putting me on.
Trees, brush and bushes don't make a sound."
"Oh yes, they do." "All right, they make sounds, I know:
wind does it, or birds, or squirrels. But not them, never *them.* Do you
    think so?"
she asks—and it's the asking part that tells me, she believes.

# Yom Kippur in Montana

Here where the light, the light
crashes with breaking beauty on the yellowing
leaves of the quaking aspens, the mountains still
ache with summer, a golden hush
holds in the blue steeps before onslaughts of winter.
I am burned with the gold,
am fled up the blue steeps into the very eye of the sun,
am the sun itself in the blue steeps.

Sawtooth mountains tilt below, Colorado goes under,
Texas slips sideways—into what Gulf—
Florida shimmers, the Keys—to what kingdom—disappear
and the sea flows phosphorescent.
Afric shores gleam, Maraketch, and everlasting sands,
Khartoum and O! Egypt,
The Negev, dwarf olive trees, and then Jerusalem,
minarets and synagogues, bazaars, a wall,
streets of sudden turning, cries, hubbub
there, where I come into my own.

But here,
in sentimental citizenry with everybody else, I am this
American: polyglot, always home-yearning:
for Israel, *my* Ire'd land, *my* ol' sod, *my* old country.

But I cannot speak the Hebrew in the streets,
my tongue cleaves or stutters. Stranger in that homeland,
soul-slain upon those alien hills.

Yet heart-speaking, lifted over voids.

Soon every larch in these familiar mountains will flame
like a sword, striking me blind with gold and splendor.
The world is one home and one splendor,
one long land
beautiful to beholders, scarred and sacred

in one light. Here the Clark Fork, geysers and pines:
also a Jordan, another Zion, more milk and other honey.

A Jew, part-time and far-gone,
but whole once a year, and immoderate
because of the Light. The Light
that even in unbelief gives courage,
bestows countrymen,
grants visions
and wings.

# Tree of Northern Lights

Wicked before this witness tree, at sinful ease. Sacrilege
of cool comfort. Your atheist too hotly disbelieves.
Our cynics hold to privilege:
they could not care less. And my Jew pleads accommodation and leaves
Whose God is Who to scroll work scholars. . . . I care no more
than nature may allow—not without the thought
that summer sifts with balsam through a clattering door—
and hang heretical complaisance on blasphemed boughs, fraught
with baubles, trinkets and geegaws. This idol of the wood
fits faithless worship and serves some good.
     Frosted grapes and crystal apples: forbidden fruit
of primitive arctic victory. They suit
extravagance of August, remembered to a fault. A gayety of Scandian
  trolls
weighs from pine needles, quite right for laughter
converted from witches and fears. Gingerbreads are dire sweetmeats.
Clefted in that frozen Pole-star, a gremlin lolls
near the very top, high-jinx giving sway to joy: after
foil and flake and brazen tongues of tapering light,
pinned aloft and grinning, it caps this Norseman's triumph. Conical
  redemption of cold.
Artifice of bells, globes, peppermint stems—and the bright
spikes of green leaves: memories of old
orchards of July. Acorns are succulent pears, and glass balls answer
gorgeous appetite. Toys strew our ground of satisfaction, feats
of fond duplicity in deep December. Abundancies of ripest life.
     If He had not been born at solstice, some other entrancer
would cheer the season: bawling infant god, rife
with the warm and saving south. And worth
this tree, this promise: these wizardries of a necessary North.

     I doubt the single Word at this late date, but set
festooned lanterns on a middle branch and share the hope of seeing
spring before summer once again,
a convict of crocuses in the glen
outside. Anthropolemical praying
for those who go a-Maying

ahead of times and will not fret
because they scant one Son's sole being.
      Birthdays are happenstance.
Such knowledge, such forgiveness. No dance
for dancing's sake? A hymn of
heart's delight? Ritual aching love
whirled and sung beneath glittering fir.
      Pendant imaginations stir
us to the quick. I also cleave
to what was born of every ancient Eve.

<pre>
                              m
                              y
                              t
                              h,
             frost of      cascade
                hoar-           of icicles
               dolls,          shimmering
             apples and          tinsel and
             remnant               weathered
          Let                          moss
                              e
                              n
                              d
                              u
                              r
                              e
</pre>

    to a timeless and evergreen winter's cure!

# this Now is blazing cold as Then was living heat

Ice light in July: shin-deep masses of seedpuffs
    heaped like snow mounds. Crystal chips
    of clover sheen. Downslope, a sun's imagination. Cut harvest hay
    lies in drifts on bare stripped fields. Tumbleweed scuffs
    across white roadglare. Where a hummingbird sips
    marigold, blinds New Year's Day. Midsummer blows the highway
    a blizzard dust ripped from ditches and dunes. Laggard lark caught
in a gusty wind.
    This sun westers backward or ahead? Trick of the Janus mind.

Burnished sky of frozen blue: remote Montana noon
    gleaming fury as at 30 below. Reckless early moon
    now as then. Live brooks leap at broken planes of beach—
    shorn and porous banks in the junctured light, not out of reach
    of willed December. Duplicate shadows heave and crack on stream
    shores, bouldered floes hazing into geysers in a mist of sunbeam.

The split year gone,
    or coming on:
    parasols of dandelion, or storm of snowflake. Struggling bird.
    Hyaline skies. Blistered icebergs. What's that heard
    now—fevered chinook sliding from Cascades near an Oregon coast,
    or remembered or prophesied blast of Canadian rage? The most
    of each pulses and confounds: dazzling August is winter,
    as February's snowfield was a sudden summer lake. Lest we
splinter
    the year into seasons, die in extremes,
    this Now is blazing cold as Then was living heat, in steadfast
temperature of dreams.

# The One That Got Away

In five feet of fast river we were on intimate terms,
myself bent double trying to hornswoggle him into the net,
and he with a head that seemed half the size of my own,
wagging it, tugging on the Mepps lure, which he'd taken instead of
    worms,
the treble hook caught in the corner of his lip, set
precariously, one spar of it. The great old massive brown
trout pulled powerfully, shaking, backing off, stripping line again.
I could neither play him much longer nor slip
him tail-end into the net, as the book says.
I grappled him toward me, once more, straight in
and he tugged, pulled, wagged, gaped, shook again,
hit the net rim—and was gone, probably to one of the bays
nearby, wary and sulking in the deep shade of the bank-side pine tree
to the right.
                Will St. Peter or some Judaical gate keeper
or Muslim or Buddhist or Tao net reaper,
glare eyeball to eyeball, head to head, with me?
(It was not his relative size, finally, or his brawn
but his age that made for likeness. So: all along
didn't I contrive to give him his chances to be free?
Did I knock the rim on him, loosening the prong?)
Will I, in turn, any day now, soon, be drawn
by the great treble hook and, rather than succumb,
suddenly pull, shake, strip out line, leap like a rainbow, quite out
of character, wagging my head, backing off, backing off, grim, dumb,
unbelievably desperate to win the eyeballing, showing no doubt
about surviving one more time? Not so full-bodied, not so stout
but shrunken, dull-colored, gaunt so,
will I nevertheless, with no homage, be let loose, an old fool
fled again to a dark, brooding, covert pool,
accidentally on purpose set free again?
                        Will I so much want to?

# Montana Young

Our children grow, leave, and don't come back.
Somewhere else they go. It's the stupid lack
of labor. Shouldn't say "stupid": I meant that fate
is inept and misspoke my feeling. In their teens and twenties
they leave at a steady rate
because here is no state of plenty,
only woods and uplands and rivers and lakes
each one has had to lovingly forsake.
They're not seeking fame,
but they go all the same.
They say, "We have to make our living."
Maybe they're back for ten days of summer or at Thanksgiving—
a pittance of return.
Mothers and fathers seethe and churn
in the hollow solitude they leave
behind, the next worse thing to grieving.
    They're very like ancestors out of the past,
leaving natal land, to cast
themselves in a different, almost foreign place. French or Finn,
Irish, German, Norwegian—these young are doubly kin
to their own grandfathers. Why come this far in time and space
to run again the same—yes, stupid—race?
    And so our boy is in Ohio or Nebraska, far from the Flathead,
and our girls watch streams of Chicago or San Diego traffic instead
of the Bitterroot or Yellowstone.
And we—you and I—are alone.
And mine and my neighbor's son and daughter,
far from the Skalkaho, Lolo's summit, or the Clearwater,
feel even more bereft
than those they left.

# Hear Ye and Harken—Another Kind of Fire Rages in the West

What brass! masses of maple trumpet the sun!
Yellow and gold hurrahs crackle this air:
orange hosannahs, copper and bronze, ignite and stun
the slopes. Listen: clarion larches stagger on, blare
every south ridge. Bells of sibilant aspen hisper in cricks
and corners. Wood winds: blazing cottonwoods chord
the draw below, alto poplars trill noon. (And sticks
of late blooming saxi-phrage pipe the undergrowth, almost unheard.)
And there and then, and there again, the steady green
bass viols of pines pines pines thrumming
the view: colors and codas, rampant choirs, forests of seen
music: mahler in the mountains, handel in the hills: autumn
of fierce-fired orchestras. Loud melodious consummations boast
the drumming in our head: scorch our eyeballs: burst our mid-most

# Better Not Go

In the dry and dire cold, sunshine is not yellow
but white—a sort of gleaming icelight at zero.
Even the sky, when clear, turns cold albino
blue, pale, deadly pale. If there is snow,
crystal flakes are keen-edged and cut so.
When mercury slumps to thirty below,
neither oil nor blood will flow
outdoors. Better not go.

# Section II

# Hyde Park
## (1966)

1

It was one more funeral. Wreaths were hung.
His proper poets were dying around the world, too young
to compose anything but themselves for death: no time like then
for elegies of fragrant grief. And no lilacs yet.

Good grey poets seemed indifferent when
the news came in. The long train
struggled up the coast; the great sun set.
Who dared to claim a special pain
while war went on? Stars and moon fell
on other shoulders, a blinding sky
glowed prophetic over Los Alamos, twilit hell
bridged the Rhine, and Iwo Jima lay hulking in the sea. To die
just then was to add one figure to a long row
of numbers. He failed in Georgia sunlight—and now
arrives at death's majority. There is a dew,
long past April, upon the grass among these trees he knew.

2

Give us this day
our fluent ease:
heroic couplets to redeem the time,
a spray
of evergreen music, one resurrecting phrase,
tentative talent like a tongue to please:
no praise of prose set to rhyme
and pressed in margins to deceive
it into form—but new bud of laurel—a surprise of bays—
and the hope of poetry in a single word's reprieve.

*Cape and cigarette holder and the jaw tilted up.*
*Our face to the world. If he stood upon infirmity,*

> *his law was a poise grown to grace*
> *and he reached the rostrum like a pulpit, preaching*
> *Dutch valor. It was not what he said exactly*
> *but exactly how he looked.*


Were vast pluralities moved?
They voted as they loved.

> *Wan like the ghost of Wilson at the last, his heart*
> *pled hemorrhages before the brain, while he brooded*
> *a peace that never came. It is not the gaunt*
> *conclusion we recall, though how a man is haunted finally*
> *counts.... Other likeliness is best.*

> *He calculated the nation in thirds and saw it*
> *whole. Some selfish few would clip an eagle's wings*
> *to feather private nests—but power*
> *was a public flight: and a hundred thousand birds*
> *of war grew global wings, after infamy.*
> *More likely yet—in mischief, with his broadest smile*
> *for first settlers, greeting dar-*
> *lings of the land as "Fellow Immigrants"*
> *in their exclusive hall.... And not too proud to confess*
> *sleepless nights with Marshall out of the country: as on a*
> *    clear*
> *fair day in Africa, he lunched with a sandwich in his*
> *    hands,*
> *rumpled hat cocked on his head and a commanding*
> *    general on the running board.*


Never was there Hail to such a Chief
while seig heils sounded overseas.
In nightmare, avuncular weight vanquished the thief
of our dreams, who fled him down dim corridors, and burned. No
    frieze
for that victory in the mind, before the fact? . . . Cast
him in bronze, mantled like his cape—he wore
it well at that, right to the last.

Or what's a President for?

> *There are no perfect heroes. He had his self-concern,*
> *human after all. But he might have chosen patrician*
> *retirement with his stamps and sailboats. He kept another*
> *rendezvous.*

This was the only fear he had to fear—
sudden eventuality, no last elation.
The voice fades on air waves of the past, streets renamed here
and there. He lacks his celebration.

> *He should have gone explosively to death, slumped*
> *in a theater stall—or been rifled like our younger one*
> *who fought the war he led. We cry no memorials*
> *to a private sufferance ... and forget.*

He had the affinity
for office fit to the dignity
we gave.
The grave
he lies in holds a man
noble republican
beyond parties of belief
in democratic grief.

3

Pity is unrequired in this park.
Lilacs grow from marble. By the dark
and ceaseless river all words are music, and assuage.
Gone the tumult. Gone the rage.
And these gone years are long.
For his too quiet rest—one belated song.

# Omaha Beach
## (1994)

Boom tide. Land danced crazy
after scud and swell. We hovered. Hid
in hot and staggered sand. That whole morning
dueled for dunes. Then, one certain cliff.
Shores were blistered. Fled inland:
tiny towns, black wreckage in hedgerows. But horses of heaven
trampled the tree tops.
Where's my platoon?
In that sea-smooth green where whitecap
crosses wash them clean. Buried with fathers
from the other war. Hallow them
not, we've heard it before. At this late
date, let us walk long windrows, the teeming
silence of a cool free beach.

# February: American Christmas

1
In winter light, pictures on a class
room wall, reflections under glass,
clarify the season:
here the fabled Father of his country,
there the crucial Savior of the union.

And our reason
these days of birth to share in schooled communion
is mutual baptism, or a being methodized together. We
have our right to some mystery
of selves on selves joined by History
                                        alone.
It's what we have in common.

2
*Twenty-second Day*
The firm mouth, bitter lips, a wigged high
forehead. Icy temperament that freezes us off. But I
appraise implacable eyes, pledged to know
this generating father of ourselves.
                        Not at the prow
of that dory over the Delaware, crossing
in the cold and famous night—though alone there
he gives connection. But lurched in Jersey retreats, bossing
his bedraggled army back and forth, hitting and running in bare
escape to hit and run again. Ignominious and cunning Alexander
through the years of mad dedication, the harsh commander
suffering his desertions and easy scorn.

But he was the nation coming to be born
out of monotonous defeats to one
bright Virginia victory. Imperious triumph won
in ardent peril: long meaning of the land. He knew that, without son
himself, siring a nation.

And we are with him now, in late celebration

of the man apart, lofty and aloof,
high rebel with a cause for fated proof:
determined in that grim and firm-set mouth
from bleeding Valley to placid Vernon in the south.

More than kingly, Presidential! With a hot
temper of some pride the cool eyes did not
show us before we looked to see. His a rage
to found, without the old world's sin of self-investiture. No sage
gazing out for Stuart's stern inspection;
not meant for boys and girls ungrown
but men and women come to know and own
him,
in dim
February reflection.

3
*Twelfth Day*
This deepened face that has appeared
to worshipers of a hundred years
lurks in its black and virile beard
and draws dumb adoration. It wears
a look that harrows our delight, and may contain
judaical imaginations from Abraham to Christ.
                                        Vain
to seek him anywhere apart
from warm impassioned eyes and the heart
melting the features in deliquescent gaze
of love and pity? Why, he also was a man, caught in a maze
of simple ambition. Did he not yearn to succeed
somehow, to earn a name, a place, a deed
for himself, even to calculate a course,
whimsical and filled with native horse
sense, welcome to a western crowd?
No providential luck allowed
to bring a homemade hero to the head of a house
divided?
        So then, he learned more than he knew he knew
or relearned it after a certain early pose,
and it was pity and a brooding humor that saw him greatly through.

"Wel-l, shooting won't do him any good,"
he said about the sleeping sentry he excused:
a wise crack out of civil dilemma, with the blood
of too much war he thus refused . . .
and a strict epitaph for assassination.
The perfect martyr, through a procrastination
of character grown beyond his dreams at last.
"Saving these states" and "freeing the slaves" and turning the past
to a future. He died in a blinding flash
just when he had to: before revilement and the dash
of expectations sure to follow.


He shall not perish while we hallow
him in all our ways, by of and for
us. And we come to him before
we do the other, suffering children of the on-
going republic, whose History is a religion
more than our churches are. There in the kind
corner of the room, above the flag perhaps, we find
him on secular days of the week, and today
in ceremonious attachment.
                        Late, the winter gray
outside the window is dark and light, less
light just now than dark, fitted to great forgiveness.


4
They are our Christmas season! half-way
between Fourths-of-July.
                      Now, New Worlds may
claim Old Testaments, bound in native leather:
a prophetical franklin, jefferson and adams getting together
at last, and dying on that same great day.


Inviolable Washington high over them all.


Or emerson as Moses, his imperative call
like a psalm to young David thoreau.
And andrew jackson our John the Baptist, though
here, and by then, naturally involved with banks.

But Lincoln, precarious conception of nancy hanks,
grown to a Gospel of love and strife
culminates our rite to life.

Through springs and firecracking summers we move
past falls to purified winters of love.
Not without wrongs and violent contest,
doubts, and a last hope to be blest.
                        This is the whole world's final country
                        vast sanctuary without a steeple.
                        World enough to pray for, land and sky
                        and chosen time to be its people.

# Can't Make Up My American Mind

Suddenly biennials burst into October,
straight wood stems lifting square flowers and sober
rectangular blossoms, sprouting full bloom in front yards
and all along roadways: red and white and, naturally, blue placards
calling loud attention to themselves. All day
"Look at *me*. Look at me!" they say,
meaning, O what a daisy!
Yes, yes, she's a lovely rose, and he's a sweet william, and hooray
for all of us, and isn't it crazy?
(Sometimes I have a thought, Do
they close their petals at night? No,
you see them in your headlight glare,
still there,
exhaling carbon dioxide, or poster ink, in the dark
pungent political air.)
They're brightest in the morning, stiff and prim and stark
and glistening with dew. You could say
it's a Montana Indian summer we have, like a second hay
cutting, every two years. But that isn't true,
it isn't Indian and it isn't summer, neither will do—
though the season is heating up some
before the first Tuesday in November. Come
midweek, there'll be a killing frost, striking them down
all at once: in every county lane, on all the streets in town,
as if there were a simultaneous universal blight
wilting them clear to their roots, clean out of sight,
carrying them off where they have to go
on the night's cold wind of election returns. I don't know
exactly if, every two years, they're a sight for sore
eyes, in all their high-blown colorful bravado, or a sore
sight for eyes that want a landscape bare
of upstart puffery, stripped of these periodic weeds of rare
hypertrophic self-praise. Hard to decide. Am I kind? Un-kind?
Can't make up my American mind.

# Section III

# Raincoatéd Victory
## (After the statue of Clemençeau by François Cogné)

1
Fallen from the ministry and raised to a pedestal
under a shade of trees near the Rond Point, darkened
beneath the host of leaves.

A greened-over statue, bronzed by conceit
to a radiance more sunned than the
four glittering horses leaping from the tops of Pont Alexandre.

2
Here's for tailors: shoes Marshal Foch scorned to wear,
leggins, a wind-creased army waterproof with five rows of plain
    buttons,
a rainhat; for his appointment, a rumpled scarf.
from the wrist, where the right hand falls into the coat pocket,
hangs a poor cane.

Sculptors: a thrust foot forward.
the left arm down a long calculation to the covert fist, silent
against the thigh, and unconfessed.
hooped-barreled body and a short neck to a broad head.
wild flag of petrified mustache, full and negligent above the lips.
eyes: liquefied with
seeing.

3
This piece of work, a kilometer from the Louvre
as the crow flies or the tourist walks
a straight gait
up the avenue
under the shade of trees, darkened
beneath the host of leaves.

On a rock ledge, tangled with weak ivy, his pedestal

Spearing the shadow like the promontorial bow of a, yes, ship
Over a sea of time.
In the morning the sun reaches his shoelaces
but after noon, he's scarcely visible.


Blazed stare melted on some distant point
Of triumph and—
amid the dull mortars whoofing death,
bulldog guns of deadlocked wars—
Inburst of glory for a man of no ideals
but facts, a hard old french—
Man.


4
But unknown Cogné has him in the moment transcending habit,
that compassionating paleness
exploding through the purple dye of blood
(illuminating ichor raised to eyesight and brainlight)
this one time:
walking in a mud swollen with the black flowers of hair
and the delicate pink rose of upturned flesh,
in all probability, not knowing, just then,
this slipt forever moment,
what
        he was.


5
But Cogné knew, this once upon
his time, making a statue the tailors in the street hardly see
no less believe. One pretty piece of work that in all probability
wasn't even the man, the real man, at all:
With the sad molting gaze
And the walking through the sponge of mud, under a rain like nails,
The amortizing pupil limned to the quick
By solar pity; and therefore translated—
Glowering down the gloom, with brusque and urgent love.
        and shoes Marshall Foch scorned to wear, leggins,
        waterproof, buttons, scarf,
        that poor cane hanging down

and the crumpled halo of rainhat.

6
And tiger eyes . . .
burning victory and benediction!
he had to live
              just to make the statue possible.

7
For Cogné: a manoeuvre
and a sky-arc of sunrays.

but always
There,
under the shade now, beneath these leaves:
Heavy leaden ghost,
                  ready for instant golden light, and dumbfounded
Cognition.

# The Obscenity

Briefed the day before: so, when we came to camp that spring
I expected everybody, regulars and replacements, to exclaim
mothaf-sonofabitchenbastards, that frictionless string
of reflexive automatic GI profanity, placing blame
on any handy gremlin or wrongdoer, easily hated
especially when prepared for. Where every other effing word was an
    article
of wearied belief in the designated suffering fated
to each of us, now there was a sudden hush, without a particle
of breath, no less speech. Champion cursers walked dumb.
Looks, yes; and shakes of head at skeletons, living and dead;
and crook'd fingers on M1s, Brownings, unholstered 45s, indexes fumb-
ling at every trigger: American Jews and gentiles straining to be led
to just one remaining German guard, oven-keeper or overseer. But
    none,
of course, remained—not one soul to blast back to kingdom gone.

# Winter at St. Légier
## (1971)

Every Sunday, just after church, the punctual Swiss
come from town to the firing range.
They shoot dutifully: side-arms, rifles, automatic
weapons. They are not aiming at apples.
They bring in and stack the targets
again in a long clapboard grange.
Then they go home.
The silent snow covers the fields the rest of the week.
On the electric wires over the white ground black
crows sit, studying the dead Germans who never came.

# Passing By
## (1990)

Once I actually lived here, taking Swiss things
seriously: did my kids really have to take German classes?
would my raise be automatic year after year, all my earnings
safe from inflation? were hiking trails getting over-built, passes
black-topped everywhere? Now I am back, a true
tourist. I hear the new old questions: should English be
the second language? are the perch bellying-up in blue
Lac Léman? will winter slopes become so crowded that to ski
we'll need traffic lights? *Mon Dieu* and *Gott im Himmel.* I do not care.
This is not even my half-country anymore. Even, by now,
my whole one isn't quite mine. I am too old to get worked up. It's fair
to say, I've always been a visitor, all over, but didn't know.
Pave from Wengen all the way to the Jungfrau and erect a copter
   hangar:
I'm only passing by. But how I loved the earthen trails and took joy in
   anger.

# Geneva: The Grand Quai, 1851

I believe we are looking east, in the print:
along the esplanade, which is really half side-
walk and half-quai. There is a glint
of gold-spattered sun on Lac Léman to the right, and splendid
four-storey apartments to the left, with lampposts down
the middle of the way. They lean the eye to a diminutive throng
in the distance, who are looking at a lake steamer anchored in town,
the novelty of mid-century, festooned with flags hung
on masts that no longer matter. All that occurs in the background,
   where
other delicately red-tiled apartment houses stretch from
the lake's rounded end a long fair
distance beyond our view. We have probably come
upon a Sunday. Or is it the peace that seduces?
                              In the foreground
a man is unloading something from a dray
at a storefront: there is a shop sign one feels bound
to make out—*Laiterie,* or *Librairie,* but the light of this day
won't tell if it's milk or books, a banal mystery
of the Geneva print. Steeping into it hypnotically,
I correct the time to late Saturday, spring or fall.
Two or three solitary workmen carry
packets on their shoulders, one is in shirtsleeves; so is a lad on the wall
of the quai, gazing at the steamer. But a couple, who tarry,
are too elegantly overclad for summertime. Still,
it can't be winter, there are hazy blobs
of leafy trees on the other side. So, it is a pastel
late September or early October morning, with cerulean dabs
of beneficent sky and delicate cloud. Nothing threatful.

No, nothing foreboding in any part of the scene.
A day of easy Jura breezes, airy, without heat,
comfortable, gentle, deliciously serene.
A high point of civilization. Part of me goes out to a few
laborers—who don't seem to be working too hard, though.
(Why, in the ideal, is *any*one straining or burdened?) And I mew
and muse, a five-year-old child in one of those close-in top-floor flats:

of a family not wealthy, but *bien aisé* as the French say,
only (but superbly) well-to-do. I peek out of one of the slats
of our shutters at the steamer, in sweet wonder. Across the way
how beautiful all existence is. I shall never know
it more exquisite and never be more at home in the world.


Note the yellow of the shutters of many windows, the yellow
awning over that perplexing shop, a cunning splash of sun on the
    furled
jacket held across his knees by the wall-sitting boy,
and the light-strewn skirt of the lady of the tarrying couple. Joy
in union. And how the lines of wall and of houses converge
in the background, joining throng and steamer. And how the lampposts
lead the eye down the middle to merge
with the rest in clear perspective. The formal and memorialized
    moment stamped
in history, forever caught in an urn-
like fixity that eluded me until I fell, headlong and heartwide,
into it.


    Will I be trusted to go to the baker's for a *baguette* not burned
unduly underneath? When I go, I shall certainly slide
down the first-floor bannister. Will we all have an excursion
on that very steamer tomorrow, or is my mother wary of soot and
    noise?
Father really wants to go himself, to try the new version
of the trip to Montreux, using me as an excuse. All boys will be boys.
This is what we look forward to on a Sun-
day, treasuring all the holidays of quiet good
living, there in unalterable Geneva of 1851.


I have been given back my life, have been stood
at the expectant window, by—whom? An artist of some fame?
Unsigned, it does not say. This composed antecedence,
splitting my eye globes, this picture of life beyond all credence
now, was not thought important enough for the man to put a name.

# Section IV

# Birds of a Fin and Fish of a Feather

The feathers of birds are like scales of fish,
and scales are feathers. Hawks swim up as they wish,
and manta rays swoop under. Fidgety turtledoves quiver in high
  pools—

fluttering angel fish are equally fickle in schools.
Billed pelicans plunge out of green sight,
and flying fish resume blue flight.

# Hawaiian Fable

A cool day at the beach under skies scudded
by a Kona wind. Making mud dikes, ramparts of dried
sand, with clam-shell buttresses on tiny
towers. A momentum of zeal—
also chill swimming that day. Craft of art
and cunning of science, because of sun denied.
  Across an isthmus five yards wide, our long thin
ditch split that spit of shore
between the calm lagoon bays. Suez
and Panama, and bridges everywhere. Real
walls of caked mortar, granulated turrets,
parks and promenades, castles and canals. Wanton sin
of conjured empire—and peopled by Lilliputian souls?
Such delicate architecture before the tide
turned. Sculpture was a vast and temporary frenzy.
The clouds blew off, and a late last kiss
of sun fell upon the outworks, blooming in bronze light.
However, the souls could not be seen. Peninsular
silence: nothing stirred on the locks and causeways, swept
by declining rays. Evening
brought miniature monsters of sand-
crabs, with great radar
eyes, dubious. What good those streets and reservoirs? Still
we stepped
gingerly. Next day no vestige of anything a-tall.
Craters of footprints on the land,
from giant Japanese fishermen out to cast a net beyond
the isthmus reef. Our world was never made.
  On the beach we played
touch football, pig's bladder tag.
Hydrotherapy for Brobdingnags.
The water warmed. We swam, of course.
That was the life. Nothing to brood
beyond our interlude
of waste demonic force.

# The Frogs of Kauai

Every night the frogs hop out of the bush and die
on the highway. They seek the warm roadbed
of cool evening and are flattened to asphalt
by revolving wheels of traffic. Gods drive cold chariots. The frogs never
  cry
out. In the early morning, quite dead,
their paws are like tiny hands in frozen protest. Whose fault?
After night's utter
silent slaughter,
a leading question. Prolonging unnatural heat-comfort, they came to
  death.
But I am touched by little fingers. Soundlessness chokes my breath.

# Spacesurfers

Just so spacesurfers will tack and veer
later: rocketing on higher seas, past cloudbanks and comet-
coral, cresting invisible waves of visible light
on a chip of unsplinterable alloy.
Straight ahead of other breakers, stellar toy
in solar wind and cosmic surf, coming on
as fast as they can stand it: on the leading edge of stark
amplitudes: down infra-red frequencies: in the burst white
glare of absolute speed. And they will slip and curve
upon those zenith waves, dare to dance and turn
along one curling wall of ultra-violet foam,
glissading through magnetic spume,
plunging toward galactic beaches, in the flume
and spray, the wash and swell of sky time.

But that spindrift surge, that steepening climb:
no more than this now, before our saltdimmed eyes:
these jocund riders,
sure of hands feet platform and the prize
of flight itself, infinite coasting.
Trust wood and plastic spars and most the buoyant
will, willing to ask what is it more, up there, we want
than what we so have here and now?

The lift! The sea-borne quaking!
and that gift-shore ahead, worth all the psalms
of futures. These running seas!
sand and the mind-blowing palms—
harbored *here,* for present taking.

# Tropic Trees

Palm fronds, ribbed and symmetrical,
are feathers,
blown ruffled plumes
of birds about to fly.
Not trees but giant condors
straining in weather
to be free again,
preening their winds in Hawaiian sky.

Visible roots striding,
the walking-trees of Kauai walk
in place. Amid the copra tree tops,
coconuts are genitalia under shameless limbs.
Monkey pods are mimics,
waving leaves like hands in the welcome wind.

And the murmur of tamarack
on the high seacoast
is almost talk.

The trees are birds, beasts and man
striving interspecies
between animal and moss.
Like the cursed sexes
seeking union if they can,
they lift up: send love through space:
and, standing, move and speak.
They know no loss.

# The Cook Islands Christian Church,
## Raratonga

Singular vanity of white straw hats blazing below
on dark Polynesian heads: luxuriant crowns. The Queen
herself snores in the corner. She wakes, mops her brow,
roused for the Maori singing, eyes open to listen. I think none

of them is here for God but the old men penitentionally dressed
in black suits and dark ties, and one old old woman mumbling
into a worn-out hymnal. A nine-year-old blessed
with lustrous hair has popped out her big barrette, fumbling

with it, making it into a blindfold. A teen-ager
raps his head rhythmically on the bench before him in soft
hyperactive madness. I forgive him. There is not a wager
of real sin here. Up in the balcony, high in the loft,

I know. Only the polyphonous singing shatters the torpor, redeeming
the Redemption. And the flamboyant hats, setting each apart:
I-am-I answering the great I Am, proclaiming
born-again pagans in the depths of their gorgeous hearts.

# Section V

# Lake Powell, Arizona

    Am not struck dumb, am not fear-
ful here, where turreted rock is what gives the world
mass, and astonished battlements withstand sunbolts
on sandstone doors flaked off to nowhere: to *now-here.*
Sculpt and rounded eyes stare open-lidded, curled
in stone. Steadfast jolts
of clockless time spellbind puny visitors.
Granite dinosaurs guard fiery heights, diabolos balance locomotive
    boulders, the sheer
walls are headlands and amplitudes for
no creatures that ever lived or were imagined or took flight in this
    planetary starkness sufficient unto itself.
    Am not struck dumb, will not from my own grace fall
to serious insignificance. And am not perversely happy to salute
fortresses of silence in primal mockery of anything, anything at all.
    Interior coastline closing back on itself, flowing in these brute
myriad canyons, under mammoth arches, lapping at the great doors,
steepening a sea of no silt or sediment
but crystalline through and through to the very floor
of the high and deep rock: life coursing through death,
buoying explorers and wonder-ers, ourselves sent
on triumphant excursion: yes, our breath
caught in original joy, eyesight split into fierce visions.
    Am not obliterated but quickened
by beginnings. And by beauty that is a collision
of earliest sun upon foundations. Am not dumb but loud
in the joy of blood fluent and thickened
inside my bodied earth: I am this clear bay
of water among this staggered rock, in this bright uncowed
bastion of
        the First Day.

# Cannon Beach

A squadron of sandpipers buzzes the beach.
They skim the wet after-tide and reach
the most recent salt margin where they land
and feed. They move so fast and deftly over the sand
that they seem to be flying or gliding yet.
Are they eating sandflies or baby crabs where it is still wet?
They are pecking at their own reflections in the moist mirror of the
    bay:
at their perfect selves underneath, just as quick—and voracious—as
    they.

# In Portland, Oregon

This line of winter rain
drops is a string of beads hanging
from the gnarled branch of bare oak
above the deck outside, above the window

we look through: the dark spar leafless and plain,
the beads luminous balls on the underside of the bough
aglow with passing sunbreak.
These delicate globes are lit white, then gold: spangling

in the shaft of sun, tinily aglitter, scintillant. The stiff
spar holds aloft the miniature lights. December's gift.

# Section VI

# Fleeting Thoughts in Montana at 48° below Zero, with Wind-Chill, at the Age of 66

Do not go light-clothed into that cold day
but bind longjohns, wool shirt, sweaters and jacket on your girth,
and sputter and rage at the specter of decay.

Remember that, in time, this is not the month of May
nor that, in space, you are Down Under, as in Perth.
Do not go light-clothed into that cold day.

Laggard to the mail box, trudge wary, try not to inveigh
against low pressure that in the Gulf of Alaska had its birth,
and sputter and rage at the specter of decay.

Note unamazed that in your high blue spruce a Canada jay
sits steady on a bough and cocks his head in creature mirth.
Do not go light-clothed into that cold day.

Tighten your gloves, pull in your neck, do not cough, or bray,
lest vocal cords twang frozen and most verily hurth,
and sputter and rage at the specter of decay.

In your dotage unexhilarated, feel the strict air pierce through your
    clay
though you walk slow, unsteady, hunkered down for all you're worth.
Do not go light-clothed into that cold day,
and sputter and rage at the specter of decay.

# Between Garrison Junction and Alberton, Montana

The light glows green for Go
but go where?
My hands are palsied on the power steer-
ing. I need a sign—not this traffic signal or that One Way arrow,
but some place name, a declaration—Two Dot, Ekalaka—that gleams
    human in this air,
so spookily moted around the blinking signal, upon the white arrow
    and against the dumb billboard that I fear


all I see is apparition merely. Weird, weird. The mercury lamps don't
help, blue-eyed ghosts on iron stilt,
while that marsh light over the city ahead
warns me in neon that I won't
like cotton candy, the carnival bulbs of used car lots, the sickly guilt
of one more night time's end of this world. Who's dead


exactly, mummified on dragster strips at one in the morning? I am.
    Garrison Junction's east,
seventy-two winding miles to a service station like a moon port, three
    roadside bars and a ruck of huddled
clapboard homes, Pop. 1000 in that void. What's west?
Alberton, and Spokane over the state line: a straight drive, at least,
to hear the engine hum. O manifold transmission! Five minutes ago I
    felt cuddled
in the car, headlights beaming into a vortex of quantum snowflake or
    melting meteors—a snug test


for phantom astronaut dreaming through black space. Those stars
    above the snow have no
kind of climate, though. Suns and planets are windless
in that dark. Or, now and then, some statistic of a green

world has turned itself to concrete causeways, arid lights and blank
  walls where the land has been.
Therefore: here, as good as anywhere. But haunted: mindless:
stalled on rubber tracks: in landscape, manscape: all rev'd up, with
  everywhere and nowhere in a universe to go.

# Close-Call for the End of the World

"Come and get me, you dirty rats," he cried, cornered on Labrador.
He fled. They nicked him near
Norway, and he streamed from the head wound but got
as far as the Pole before they closed in on him: not the cops but
the rats. He had taken care of the law—and machine-gunned
the trees, gassed all the little furry animals, stunned
the big game, crating them to death, and poisoned the perennials.
Except for two hippos wallowing in Mozambique, a squadron of sea
    gulls
flying off Ireland, three upside-down bats
hanging in Andean moss—and those last, judicial rats.

# Letter to the East

Dear Al, I wanted to send you a stone
but at the river edge I found a goddamn brick
instead. So here it is.
About that stone:
I was going to go up and down a bank of Rock Creek,
you know, Kitchen Gulch, the oxbow where the water
and shores bend in to the steep mountain. Well,
maybe you've forgotten. But try to remember. Anyway,
I wanted a small smooth stone for you, striated—
how's that for breaking out of my simplicity? No
deep symbolism (the water there is shallow this time
of year) about rough sides to your soul or our
friendship. Just a plain memento.
But I found this whole brick instead—who put it
there, I don't know—red-faced, chipped slightly,
frayed around the edges. I mean, the brick.

So here it is,
in a shoebox, for Christ sake. I don't know what
you'll do with it, you can't just put it on a mantle-
piece or anything like that. You can't even kick it
without hurting yourself. Don't throw it
at anybody just yet. Hide it maybe.
In fact,
hold on to it—to me—for a while longer. I'm a
man-made thing too, partly, heated in some social
furnace, and all that. Etc., etc. You know what
I mean.
Listen,
I'm still looking for a suitable stone, I'm
particular about what I search for, not what
I find. You'll just have to wait, ol' buddy;
and stop writing those hostile reviews
or I'll send you a discovered arrowhead among
the pebbles or a discounted mountain rope on sale
at the Clark Fork Sporting Goods Store.

# Unnaturalized American

He visits countryside like a jungle where the crouched tiger lily
may spring from dappled shade. Fears the stab
of sudden hummingbird. Hastens over upland fields, wary of snapping
   crab-
grass. Wild strawberries startle him silly.
Hears in open landscape a roar from dandelions: is routed by
   dragonflies:
burrows through bear grass, back to safe cities: far from avenging blue
   skies.

# Section VII

# Sonnet: The Solecism of Your Smile, or the Passionate Professor to His Love

That ineluctable vacancy between your pendant ear lobes
has launched a thousand metaphorical frigates of attention.
Let me not praise that hiatus alone, but take coordinates of your eyes
   with a strobe
light, measure all that's efflorescent on those cheeks, not to mention
the adumbration of your pillared neck and, soft and holistic,
the architectonics of your breasts, those turgid thighs,
incognizant shanks, otiose ankles and the tips of your heuristic
toes. I am at your ukase, suffering any rubric of your sighs
for the sole desideratum of your lips. What! Cast down in obfuscation?
Classic apprehension's in your glance; the furrowed simulacrum of that
   brow
crinkles at my meaning. Incunabula in the moonlight! Lest I have
   osculation
at that mouth, I am defunct! In ev'ry thy eschatology, I am milennially
   yours, especially now,
when in academical heat. Are you recalcitrant? Let me analogize you to
   an equinoctial solstice—or is that fall?—
never mind. If I'm aleatory, this impassioned jargon will render you
   unconscious, and mine, once and for all.

# Transport of Love

Two newlyweds flew, seated over foam
rubber, on a torqueless electro-welded jet.
The wing-severed, screamlined dome
of fuselage, with minimum distortion and fret,

accordionized just outside of Pitt-
sburgh, and local sylvan and aero officials,
researching ashed metal where it hit
and swatches of clothes and keyring initials,

discovered that the honeymoon was not over,
when Orpheus descended. Nothing less
among the tags of cushions on the clover
than the lovers in memorial caress.

Disastrous workers were measurably harrowed
by unexampled sight of mingled bliss:
the distance between lovers narrowed
in that welded adoration of their kiss.

Most than enough to rouse a buried dread
recovered after shovel, rake and broom:
Awe men! to the lockjawed double-head
of this ardent and premeditated doom.

# Odysseus off Long Island, Penelope in Her Duplex

Undulant marrow: hunched and snuggled
and skinned to their tines, thigh to thigh.
Forked and conjugal flesh on a bare bed
of rippled linen. When the high alarm went
off, covered her ear with the soft of his hand.

His leave toward shore. Stirred a shin, smuggled
toes to waking coasts. Her heave a sea. Sigh-
ed away the lighthouse clock: crested tides: pled
spumes and froth, the taste of salt. Breasting imminent
morning, locked his limbs from that floor of land.

Fled to the chafed cliffs: scraped sky: stark breath:
the cockles of his however heart serene. And widow's death
her negligence: quietus with coffee and toast. Keen-
ing in the breakfast nook: sufficiently slain.

# Somebody's Grandmother, Somebody's Grandfather

"What are you looking at me for, why are you looking at me?
Why are you staring,
Why are you caring,
What can the reason be?"

*"If you were I and I were you,
You'd be looking, too.
But you are you and I am I,
Then I'll be going by."*

"Why do you hurry, why do you worry
To be moving off so fast?
If you tarry, maybe we'll marry
So long as you've not gone past."

*"Oh, I wasn't moving,
I was loving
And gave myself some slack—
As soon as I knew
That the likes of you
Give me that first look back."*

# Love Story

I thought that being buried
together would be close enough. Our bones would leach
one to the next, whitely, side to side,
neck bone connected to the neck bone, thigh to thigh, etcetera.

But we could not be placed each with each,
it's against a law—the law—some law: such plethora
in one pine box! (and who knows what other
superstition?) Then how about two boxes in the same lot,

pressed against one another, whole length to whole length?
But side by side in the same wide plot
won't do either, even if I had the strength
to reach across and touch,

because how could I slip my hand through wood—
and wood again—you hutched and I hutched
apart? I should if I would but I could
n't. Better to be soft ashes, infinite bright flakes

held in a vessel for the other, then both shaken
together and taken aloft, for heaven's sake,
up high enough—and let go—out of the plane, forsaken
to cloud, sky, fused mist, up there somewhere

forever part of sheer atmosphere:
not touching, not even holding, but comingled
each to each, each in each, all particles a single
mist, unique dust, uniform air

in wedded, welded flight:
gone together—come together—in one bodiless light.

# Section VIII

# The Last Horse and My Father

The horse of the last horse and wagon in New Jersey bolts
on Willow Avenue in Hoboken in 1938, just a block
from the family store. He swerves and careens and jolts
the wagon over the curb and bounces it back
to the street, the horse wild-eyed, pounding. People have fled
into cellars, up telephone poles, across sidewalks,
fleet with fright, agile in fear, shot with dread
from the noise alone. Nothing and no one can balk
the horse. Windows slam up, the tenements are loud.
"What's hap?" "Police!" "Are there babies in the crowd?"

My father, sure-handed drayman from the old days,
slips out the door into the middle of the street,
stands there, waiting. The enormous horse, in a daze
of his own terror, bears down, wagon walloping, hooves and cleats
flailing, the people in their great scattering,
my short father waiting, with a cigarette in his lips. I see him yet.

At the intersection, only four doors away, the clattering
horse and wagon veer. That great clyde saw my father looming
in his equine eyeballs: magnified man, determined, immobile,
compact, stalwart: waiting to grab the booming
horse by halter, harness or passing shaft and pull
the demon down. Shooting sparks from pinwheel eyes,
the thick-hewn beast whirls! and turns
on a dime at Willow and Sixth. One rear wagon wheel flies
off, spinning into an iron fence, the other churns
spokeless, the great horse come to a frothing stop rather
than face the likes of my little father.

# Ethnic Jewish American in Seville
# and Toledo

1

I know what it means, that Star of David
at seven o'clock in the stained glass window
of the cathedral of Seville. *We are here,* it says, in blazing glass, the gravid
lead of the mosaics—Mosaics!—the burst light, the shadows

placed just there by a *converso* or some authentic, legal Jew.
(Either way, one has to account for permission or inspiration.
Twelfth century Spain: the land of true
catholicity, all three faiths joined in peninsular toleration.

Before the strict mania of Isabella, the expulsions
and forced conversions, here was transcendent
Church, its great soul in the stones, a monument, before convulsions,
as broad as it was high, resplendent

with unhypocritical grace. Symbolic allowance, just past dawn, for Jews
to proclaim, We were here, first and foremost). And it is clear
in the streaming light, in the glory of circumspection, the lightning blues
and whites, they still declare, *We are here.*

2

No Pyrenean gates reopened four
hundred and fifty years later for Judaic ingathering and
protection. Some few slipped in, precious coins and jewels, a store
of German silver or Antwerp diamonds their currency in hand

for perilous escape (the rest boxcar'd, without quarter,
to dire Babylon). Now an over-talkative lady guide
at the ex-synagogue in Toledo, eyes a-water,
is compassionate with touring Jews, come here from the wide

96

world's other salvations. They stand and stare
at the wall above the Covenant niche. A gilt cross
hangs aslant in the holy of holy places, in this rare
arcaded room that Moors helped erect. Gold leaf is dross.

3

Scant Jews in Seville and none in Toledo now,
not since the dispersion. (But *conversos* met in secret
connected cellars, sharing *shabbis:* like early fearful Christians bow-
ing their heads in Rome's catacombs). Gentiles may regret

and be burden-free at the same time. It is convenient.
But only when Pyrenean gates swing open and the seas flow
back, and the chapel cross comes down, and lenient
cardinals and laity do what they are still too slow

to do, and the synagogue is restored, will all the clocks of Spain ring
seven with Seville, and the sun stream upon the Star,
and cantors—with priests and mullahs—arise and sing,
*We are here* again: *We are here.*